GODDESSES OF INDIA

Lakshmi the Goddess of Prosperity

SHUBHA VILAS

Om KIDZ
An imprint of Om Books International

Goddess Lakshmi, the consort of Lord Vishnu is the goddess of wealth and fortune. She chooses good over evil and forsakes those who are arrogant and greedy. Without her blessings, one cannot enjoy the good things in life.

This makes her a popular and revered goddess of almost every Hindu family.

Once, angry with Indra, an enraged Durvasa Muni cursed all the devatas to turn old and weak. As a result, the devatas lost their battles with the asuras, who gained control over the Universe. Sad and dejected, the devatas went to Lord Vishnu to seek his help.

Lord Vishnu suggested that they churn the nectar or amrit from the ocean and drink it. This was extremely important for the gods because only this nectar could restore their youthful life.

The devatas were too weak to churn the ocean by themselves. They requested the asuras to help them. The asuras agreed. They secretly planned that they would steal the nectar and not let the devatas have it.

So, the churning of the ocean began. The ocean first threw up poison which Shiva gladly consumed and became known as the blue-throated god, the Neelkantha.

The ocean threw up many gifts from its depth. Among them, was the miraculous cow Kamadhenu, a seven-headed horse, Varuni, the goddess of alcohol, and also Indra's majestic white elephant, Airavat who had been the cause of the curse from Durvasa Muni. Both Indra and Airavat were happy to reunite and wept tears of joy.

Next emerged the beautiful goddess Lakshmi, daughter of the ocean. She was sitting on a big, beautiful lotus. In that instant, Lakshmi felt drawn towards the charming, confident personality of Vishnu, the Supreme Being.

She looked around to examine if there was anyone endowed with better qualities than Vishnu.

Some had knowledge, but no wisdom. Some had power but no compassion. Some had long lives but no auspiciousness. Some had auspiciousness but were not devotees.

All in all, the only complete personality in that gathering of all the gods and demons was Vishnu, the Supreme Lord. Vishnu's transcendental qualities made him the most desirable.

After full deliberation, Lakshmi, the goddess of fortune, accepted Vishnu as her husband. Symbolically, by choosing Vishnu as her husband, Lakshmi rejected the evil in the asuras and accepted the goodness in the devas.

Goddess Lakshmi is worshipped with great enthusiasm on the Hindu festival of Diwali. Diwali marks the end of many asuras like Narakasura by Lord Krishna, Ravana by Lord Rama and Bali by Lord Vamana. As the victory of good over evil is said to bring prosperity, Lakshmi is worshipped with reverence on the festival of lights.